Poems from a Family Man

by

John Marshall

Augur Press

POEMS FROM A FAMILY MAN

Copyright © John Marshall 2014

The moral right of the author has been asserted

British Library Cataloguing in Publication Data.
A catalogue record for this book is available from
the British Library.

ISBN 978-0-9571380-6-3

First published 2014 by
Augur Press
Delf House
52 Penicuik Road
Roslin
Midlothian EH25 9LH
United Kingdom

Printed by Lightning Source

Poems from a Family Man

Dedication

To my mother, who was a wonderful woman, and to my nephew, who passed away quite recently. I miss them both.

Contents

Preface
Introduction

Preface

John Marshall is a man who is devoted to his family. His commitment to the wellbeing and future of his five daughters is unshakeable.

He is adept at conjuring up images and experiences in a reader's mind. Effortlessly, he invites his audience to enter diverse arenas, taking us on a journey through familiar elements of human experience, and shining a light into corners that others may not always wish to reveal.

In this book his words paint scenes from nature, interwoven with a profound sense of his relationship with natural things. By contrast, he goes on to reflect on the struggles that inner life can entail, including both physical and emotional pain.

The sudden unexpected loss of his mother is painfully and honestly expressed. Being thrown into a state of deep shock was only the beginning of a long and protracted grieving process, with which many of us can identify.

His thoughts on the subjects of relationship, marriage, pregnancy, childbirth, and also infant death are represented. Then follows a fascinating window into family life.

The collection ends with personal reflections about life itself and what might lie beyond death.

Introduction

I am Scottish and was born in Glasgow. We moved around quite a bit during my growing up years, including living in Pollok, Paisley and Barrhead. I am 45 years old. I am married. I have always lived in Scotland, and I have never been tempted to live anywhere else. My wife and I have five daughters – aged 21, 20, 18, 18 and 15. We have a 14-year-old Rottweiler named Jake and a three-legged cat called Oscar.

I live with severe disability due to a bad car crash many years ago. I prefer not to dwell on this. I walk tentatively, and occasionally with assistance. My wife goes out to work. I am based at home. Although I am unemployed, I am very busy because I spend lots of time with my five girls. I do all the cooking. We don't like processed food, and I put a lot of time into making nourishing meals. I have written a cookbook using my own recipes, and I hope that this will be published in the future.

When I am not busy with my daughters and creating homemade food, I spend time writing. I started writing when I was nine years old. To begin with I wrote poetry, but when I was still nine I also had an idea for a novel. I didn't have the confidence to write the novel. Its title – a *Seven Day Hell* – came into my mind much later on. I tried often over my early years to write this thriller, but at that tender age I really did not have the confidence, and I struggled with one issue or another. In the end, I did not write it until much later on in life. I was really excited when it was published in the USA. It is now available in the UK, too.

I wrote a children's book called *Crabby Family of Crabby Cove* a few years ago. It was published soon after I submitted it.

I write most days, and I tend to have up to ten writing projects in one form or another at any one time – so it's almost non-stop! I have a few ideas in the pipeline for more novels. I hope they will emerge over time.

I am very grateful for the fact that my daughters push me to send my writing to publishers.

I love sports especially football, golf, boxing and tennis. In fact I enjoy most sports except cricket, which is a game I don't understand.

John Marshall
September 2014

POEMS

Highland joy

Holiday time! I couldn't wait
Peace and solitude just sounds great.
Me and my family went up to bliss
in a beautiful lodge. I'm glad I didn't miss
the views. They were inspiring, weather wasn't great,
still enjoyed the scenery, it was almost like fate.
We relaxed all week, we chilled and did zero.
Highland home just became my hero.
I could see the mountains. No internet to be had.
My family were tech-deprived, can't say I wasn't glad.
Went for long walks down to the loch
No pressure at all, we talked a lot.
Kids could be a bit bored, they might not go back
I would definitely return, just pack my rucksack.
One hour's drive away from my house
For once I felt as small as a mouse.
In the shadow of mountains as far as I could see
the ideal world – a vision to me.
I would live there in a flash, I'd move next day
I would settle in the quiet, the best place to be.
Never any stress, I felt my tension melt
My family saw the difference, my mood they felt.
If I get a chance, I would book it tomorrow
A repeat holiday, even if I had to borrow.
To return to my second home, chill for a week
I'd never need to search for the happiness I seek.

Learning life

Wispy whistle of a passing breeze
Used to bring me to my knees.
Wonders of nature leave me breathless
Catching the wind, just feeling helpless.
Be with nature, be at one with your own being
Never stress yourself out, know what you're seeing.
Life passes fast if you don't take time out
If you let it go by, you'll miss what it's about.
De-stress when you can, wherever available
Take deep breaths, nothing is unassailable.
Minute after minute, week after week
People are always looking, but very rarely seek.
Let the bad things pass, nurture the good as it comes
You'll benefit a lot, you'll know when it forms.
You'll find your life will be immeasurably better,
Don't sit about idle, be a go-getter.
You'll begin to smile, no matter the drama
Take all of the punches, life's a charmer.

The beauty of the view

Words don't portray the true beauty of the sights
The long winding roads, the owls at night.
The scent of fresh blooms in the early spring season
These smells appear yearly without giving a reason.
They enchant and romance you, and change your mood
Your health feels better; it's all for the greater good.
Nature can trick you, amaze and astound
Beautiful memories, birds singing aloud.
Never wish it to end, spring is my favourite season
Spring fills me with happiness for no other reason.
Small gusts of wind tantalise your senses
Spring's the time nature throws down her fences.
Almost too many changes for me to remember
To do them all justice, like a winter in December.
I would miss this season if it ceased to exist
If it disappeared like a slow lingering mist.
Seeing nature's beauty is a privilege in its own.
When you experience it once, the seeds are sown.
You will always look forward to the ever-approaching season
Deep down you'll know, you'll have your own reason.
Everyone can love certain aspects of the spring
I think myself it's a very personal thing.
Whether you love the birds, the streams or the nights,
They are all individual, they are wonderful sights.
All the other seasons are special on their own.
Yet they don't match spring for me, my imagination is sown.
The seeds are planted, infinite sights and sounds
Happy memories for me are sure to come around.

Life in time

Life itself is a complex thing
Some days you laugh, others you sing.
Just when you're happy, life tends to trip you up
People always refer to life's big tea cup.
Some days good, others bad
Laughing one day, the following you're sad.
Giving out help, trying to do your best
People make fun of you, then you feel sick.
I try to help, be a nicer guy
Some days there's no point, people kick dirt in your eye.
There are always people who take advantage
Of other's good nature, it's seen as a disadvantage.
If you're nice to people they can get suspicious
Even if you're genuine, not surreptitious.
People take their time to trust a stranger
Always feeling that they are in some kind of danger.
Apparently you never look a gift horse in the mouth
Or people will turn you over and run down south.
Maybe there is some truth in the rumour
Try to trust people a little bit sooner.
Not everyone is bad or trying to steal your money
You never know, they might even be funny.
Try to trust a person you've known for a while
At the end of the day they might make you smile.

What am I thinking?

Whatever I need to tell you
How much do you need to know?
Where has my life been?
Where will my life go?
I never feel the urge
To open up my heart
I cry or open up occasionally
Is that me making a start?
Knowing how people are feeling
Has always been my gift
I tell it like it is, and
cause the occasional rift.
People respect my honesty
They hate it when I lie
Always tell it like it is
Sometimes it's hard to try.
Don't treat someone like a kid
Be honest to you and myself
Don't patronise people
You owe it to yourself.

Being let down

Being let down is a current theme
Everyone I know crashing my dream.
Tried to please everyone, they're never happy
So immature, they should be wearing a nappy.
Lies, betrayal, sell you down the stream
Promise one thing, disappears from the scene.
I cannae win, I try my best
Doesn't help my state, I should stuff the rest.
Do my own thing and be true to me
Maybe things will be different, just wait to see.
Being torn between two people
Is like climbing an impossible steeple.
Pulling one way, and then another,
I honestly don't know why I bother.
Can't do right for doing wrong
Seems to be a familiar song.
From now on, baby steps for my sanity
Not pleasing everyone just for their vanity.

Depression

When I woke this morning
The whole world was grey.
Nobody talking,
Nothing to say.
Didn't want to leave my bed
I'd rather be dead.
It's coming to a head, I feel the pressure is on
The world is killing me, it weighs a tonne.
Nowhere to turn, no avenues to walk
People don't want to know, don't want to talk.
Living on the edge, existing day by day
Gets harder and harder, a way out I pray.
Arguing with myself, arguing with family,
Seems an endless journey, wondering who will harm me.
I've seen the doctor, drugs are the next course,
He has the solution, he's a medic of course.
He knows what he's doing, it's not a ruse
Give him a chance, what have you got to lose?
Doped up to the eyeballs, not feeling myself
I'm losing my mind, I'm losing my self.
I have to go on for the sake of my kids
Even though it feels like my life's on the skids.
I *will* carry on, I'm a determined guy
One day I'll be happy, I'll soar in the sky.

More ups, less downs

Whenever you're troubled, whenever you're down
Try to smile, it's harder to frown.
Speak to your family, phone your friend
You'll find in time the problem will mend.
Nothing is ever as bad as it seems
Everyday hopes can be tomorrow's dreams.
We all have bad days, we all have good
It's better to talk, it's no time to brood.
No matter your downs, ups aren't far away
I'm speaking from experience, I thought I'd just say.
Human beings are all destined for a bit of badness
It's part of the trials – ultimately sadness.
It's part of trials and tribulations
Forty per cent bad days, but sixty, celebrations.
I believe in the power of positive thinking
Although there are times when I feel like I'm sinking.
I try to look ahead for possibilities, and hope
It's the way to get through, a good way to cope.

Alone

Being lonely, having no one to tell,
With a mental illness can feel like hell.
I'm used to the company, someone to pass the time
It's hard to do nothing, you can hear the clock chime.
Total quiet, peace and solitude, nothing to do
Puts you on a downer, makes you feel blue.
Thinking of things to liven up your day
They don't all work, I have to say.
My dog and my cat entertain only so much
You depend upon people like the proverbial crutch.
Depression's been my constant companion for years
Multitude of emotions, laughter, then tears.
Ups and downs, highs and lows
Hard to take all the mental blows.
I go online or read a book, often it works if I go and cook.
Relaxes me greatly, takes me far away,
Lovely tasty food kills a boring day.
Everyone has a prop to rely on
Even after friends are often long gone.
Tiredness, happiness, emotionally frail and sad
Each and every day goes from good to bad.
I pick myself up when I feel really down.
Do something simple, even a walk up the town.
You never know your luck, you could turn things round
May make you feel lifted, with your feet on the ground.
The main thing in life is that you never give in
Families notice changes, they're there to raise your chin.

Full circle

From birth comes life, from death comes life
From sadness comes joy, from heartache comes strife.
Daily dilemmas, nightly fears
Still in the dark, enduring the tears.
All alone, gentle touch would be right,
But no one to speak, no closeness in sight.
Despair is real, loneliness a fright
Sitting on your own at the dead of night.
Coming to a head, getting a grip
Left too long, sanity will drip.
Compose, self heal, calm and laugh
A full life is surely better than half.
Get through the din, get through being alone
Sometimes it's so real, cuts you to the bone.
Day by day, night by night
The fear will go, the light is in sight.
Build up slowly, in a situation like mine
Life will grow back eventually, given time.

Back ache

Today I experienced a new level of pain,
I'm struggling to see what I'm going to gain.
I felt it go, I felt it move around,
Scraping my bones, an unsettling sound.
I felt very sick after, and unsteady on my feet,
I had no choice but to have a seat.

Fifteen years of osteoarthritis…
Each day I struggle more
I could write a book,
But what would it be for?
Some days it's good, others really bad,
Some days I'm happy, others very sad.
Had the condition now for so many years
The pain is so bad I've been reduced to tears.
Tried physiotherapy, acupuncture and many more,
Each treatment pointless, just leaves me really sore.
I've been told an operation is out of the question
No guarantee of success, at least not to mention.
The NHS is great. It's helped me out lots,
But when it's down to cash, it's like joining the dots.
I've been told I'll be like this for the rest of my life.
When reality hits, it cuts like a knife.

I've no choice now. Just grin and bear it.
Can't justify an operation, but it hurts quite a bit.

Suffering loss

It was an awful day – when I lost my Mum
From head to toe, all I felt was numb.
People walking by, saying their 'sorrys'
All I could think of were my own personal worries.
Time stood still, hardly a minute passed,
Visions of my Mum, through my head they rushed.
Times gone by, so happy, so content.
A life ripped away. Was it really meant?
One minute talking, having such fun
Immediately afterward, the rising of the sun.
I sat at the corner, just after she died
The world looked still, that morning I cried.
No cars would pass, no people would walk by
My tears would glisten in the bright day sky.
Went to my best friend to give him the news
All he could express were his heartfelt views.
It was nice the company I had in those first few hours
Time passed slightly faster, in companionship of ours.

The day had started so lonely, I never knew where I was
Trying to sort out my head, for a non-sense cause.

Tragedy

A horrible occurrence, that installs instant fears
Complex emotions, inevitable tears.
It comes to us all at some point or another
It happened to me, the tragedy was my mother.
Taken long before her time
Still sends shivers down my spine.
Took me so many years to bypass the shock
It was several months before I could even talk.
When eventually I did, the emotion door opened clear
Found it hard, now a new emotional fear.
Not used to sharing, relying or talking
Felt so vulnerable, thought I'd see mocking.
After so many years' ups and downs
Eventually the cure was to simply move towns.

Fifteen years long

Seventeenth of June 2006
 – a date in my head that definitely sticks…

Fifteen years after my mother had died,
We scattered her ashes, but no one cried.
Like going through the trauma all over again
Double the grief, double the pain.
For whatever reason, the decision was made
It was the correct one, nothing more was said.
My mum's now at peace, of this I am sure
My sister's decision, from her heart, it was pure.
She did the right thing, it took her a while
She knows deep in herself, think of Mum with a smile.
I'm content at last, can visit my family's grave
All memories I treasure, all thoughts I save.
Now Mum's with her kin, they can meet once more
A happier family, it's no longer sore.
I sleep better at night, I feel happier by day
This is my legacy I'm pleased to say.

Two spirits

This person is special, you constantly thought
You know she's real, affection not bought.
Keep her close to your heart, you know you must do
Don't lose her, play it real, and you won't have to.
Treat her well, say you love her every day
She'll return the compliment, you'll hear her say.
Too many people let the special one go
By being shy or pigheaded; just go with the flow.
It's about trust and being true to her in your life
She'll support you through all the trouble and strife.
You must not tell her lies or shatter her trust
That cuts through your heart with a cruel thrust.
Like all relationships, you'll have to work at it each day
The feeling you get back is heartwarming I must say.
I wouldn't swap anything for what I have now,
On my wedding day that was my solemn vow.

Commitment

Commitment's a thing we all desire
It gives a relationship a certain fire.
Along with other things like love, not lust,
Eventually we all seek a certain type of trust.
You need such things to make it last
And not to cause it to be a thing of the past.
Then your partner can go out for the night,
And you'll trust them with all your might.
Don't let the green-eyed monster come near
Or your relationship will entail some fear.
Wondering where he or she is,
Getting yourself in a terrible tiz.
So establish a trust
Be anything at all
To ensure your love
Won't wither and fall
To a point of no return.

To feel so lost, your heart would burn.

Marriage

Marriage, for some, is a wonderful thing
It makes them happy. What else will it bring?
For the occasional unfortunate it isn't so nice
Their lives are squeezed, as if in a vice.
They suffer for years
Because of a love they did once feel.
To you and me it may not seem real.
Unfortunately this trouble does exist
And it's in everyone's midst.

Some marriages are made in heaven,
And some are not.
Others are just
Easily forgot.
Yet knowing this subject
It still goes on and on.
People still do it.
At the time it surely was fun.

Some marriages are doomed to fall
Many others will bloom and grow tall.

Pregnancy scares

Heartstopping…

This day I remember, it was a day I did dread
Thought going to hospital to find out my baby was dead.
My wife was rushed there in terrible pain
I was sure the day would end without any gain.
I entered the ward, saw tears on her face
I tried to keep smiling, while my heart did race.
I asked how it went. She looked so relieved
Now having twins! Too good to be believed.
I thought I was losing a baby that day
Instead I gained another! I was elated, needless to say.

They're grown up now. Seventeen years old
Cheeky, brash, even a tad bold.
They are amazing, surprising, infuriating and crazy
I don't remember the bad times, at best they are hazy.
I remember as babies, so very demanding
I loved every minute. Just takes careful handling.

I now have five girls, they're as different as can be
They rely on me so much. Makes me get up every day.
I would do anything in life so they didn't suffer pain
I'd walk to the ends of the earth, even if I'd nothing to gain.
They are my all, they are my everything
Some days they make you mad, others you sing.

If I had choice about how to live my life again
I would not change a single thing.

Life being born

The experience itself is a wonderful thing
Watching your baby being born, you feel you could sing.
First comes the head, then comes the neck
You shake like a leaf, you're a nervous wreck.
Then the shoulders, and then the rest
The sight is amazing, that tiny wee chest.
Once the baby is totally out, you look at her face
There's no doubt you love her, your heart starts to race.
She lets out a scream, a deafening cry
It's been a long hard slog, you let out a sigh.
For all the labour can go on for hours
You comfort your wife, say she'll always be yours.
A precious bundle, totally dependent on you,
A mighty responsibility, but you will pull her through.
Her needs are huge, her routine is crucial
Your love for this child is absolutely essential.
You watch her grow, teach her things every day
When she gets older, still show her the way.

Baby Peter

I had a nephew who lived for one day
It was touch and go. All I did was pray.
Baby Peter just was not strong enough
For my sister and Peter, that day was rough.
They stayed in hospital getting him ready to say goodbye
I sat at home, and all I could do was cry.
I went to the funeral, okay at the start
Emotion kicked in as I watched him depart.
His tiny white coffin, so small, so special,
I'll miss him growing up, he would have been exceptional.
It's true what they say – memories cast in stone
Seeing my nephew buried, it cut to the bone.
I never met him, but felt I knew him
Love and emotions, from us, sent through him.
As years go by, he won't be forgotten
We'll visit his grave, no chance of oblivion.
His brothers, sisters, parents and kin
We'll cherish his memory to keep him in being
I sit late at night, wondering what he could have been
What would he be like? What would we have seen?
Much like his brother, and his sister as well?
It's all just dreams. Who really could tell?
What's done will stay done, what's past will stay past
Memories continue, they will always last.

Children

What about kids? Are they a ball?
Or do they drive us right up the wall?
Sometimes they're good, sometimes they're bad
They make you happy, but they can make you sad.
In all sincerity, could we do without?
I do not think so, of this I've no doubt.
No matter how bad the kids behave
Even seeming to drive you to the edge of the grave.
One thing's for sure like the flight of a dove
Those two feet terrors you will always love.
In my opinion, these kids I adore
Even at eighteen, when you might show them the door

There's always a place for them in your heart.
You and your kids will never really part.

Families

When it comes to families, not many can boast
With my five kids, I can boast more than most.
Always a credit, never let me down,
They make me happy, with an occasional frown.
They're still quite young, their intelligence grows,
They are all beautiful, and their kindness flows.
There's not a day goes by that I'm not proud.
Always bright skies above, never a cloud.
They continue to amaze, astound and mature
How they will fare, you can never be sure.
No matter what they do, or where they might go
I will always be proud, this I definitely know.
On my face each day the joy I feel shows
It's getting bigger as each day goes.
I always help them and try to think ahead
I want to care for them forever, I've often said.

Cooking for pleasure

I love to cook and I love to bake
My wife says I make the best Madeira cake.
My girls and I cook a variety of dishes
When it works out well, god grants all your wishes.
My signature dish is home made steak pie
Seeing the full faces puts you on a high.
I think I'm a pretty good cook,
Yet I never use a recipe book.
I make it up as I go along,
Just like a writer with his number one song.
Usually it tastes and smells so good,
If it doesn't I go into a stinker of a mood.
I am a chef at home in the kitchen
Too many helpers can sometimes cause friction.
I like some help now and again
Are the best cooks really men?
I just love to mix my cakes
They really are speciality bakes.
Chocolate orange cake, shortbread or pie
No stopping me, the limit's the sky.

I've always cooked from an early age
My mum taught me, aged nine, just as a gauge
To see how I handle the heat and the strain.
She said I definitely used my brain.
My mum believed you should be able to look after yourself
Cooking and cleaning, and creating meals from the shelf.

If you can look after yourself, you'll never go short
Household duties you can easily sort.
If you do the task often enough
It becomes easy, not tough.
Practice makes perfect, an accurate phrase
Helps you navigate through life's little maze.

Jake

Jake, my dog, a lot can be said
Loyal and faithful, our hunger he fed.
Amazing and loving, funny and mad
He keeps us all going, through good and bad.
Fourteen years old, Rottweiler cross
Struts around as if he's the boss.
You often wish they'd last forever
Pets grow with you, all of us together.
Tackles anything you throw on his plate
Strong and wilful, he is a true mate.
I dread the day he's no longer here
That's the day the whole family fear.
He would last in our memories, of that I'm sure
But for a broken heart there is no cure.
Grew up with my kids, took all their madness
Sometimes his life has been tinged with sadness.
We took him to the vet, we thought that was it
We were not sure how he would take the hit.
Thankfully he came through, relatively unscathed,
His old heart strong through the operation he braved.
We can only hope that he lasts a while
He definitely has already stayed the proverbial mile.

Putting things right

Flowers waving in a petulant wind
Strongly pushing, never rescind.
Trees look scared of the powerful force
Afraid to let nature take its course.
A lonely bag flies by in the sky
Where it ends up might be nearby.
Weather's changing, getting worse by the day
Global warming is what the experts say.
Birds soaring high in the sky
Touching heaven as life passes by.
Give people a chance, let life be lived right
No one knows the future, there is no insight.
You can't do right for doing wrong my mum used to say
She was very wise, I know, through every night and day.
People will flock to the next big thing
It always has too familiar a ring.
If we all do our best, get on with life as we can,
We can live mostly in harmony, women and men.
No one can be right all of the time
No matter what they tell you, you'll find out just fine.
It's a case of taking it one day after another
Be plain and simple – causes less bother.

Who regrets?

What happens next, when your time has passed?
When you feel like your life has gone by too fast.
Do you try to slow down or accept it's too late?
Do you look back on life? How much of it did you hate?
Have you any regrets? Any things you didn't do?
Do you hate many people? Do they hate you?
Did you wrong anybody? Did anyone wrong you?
How much were you proud? How much ashamed?
Were you responsible? For what were you blamed?
Will you leave a legacy? Will it be good or bad?
When you finally pass over, will you be happy or sad?
Life's too short for 'what ifs' or regrets
Take chances every day, hedge your bets.
You'll never know what you could have been
Get out, mix and mingle, get yourself seen.
Every now and then, do something that scares you
Laugh at yourself, people will laugh with you.
Whenever you smile, or whenever you're down
Get out and socialise, just hit the town.

The future

Everyone ponders, Is there life after death?
What really happens when we take our last breath?
Do we go to a place that is brave and bold?
Nobody knows, so many stories are told.
We like to think we'd go somewhere nice
Is that the truth once you've paid your price?
I like to surmise that there's a new world waiting
What's the alternative? Is hell really in the offing?
It's described in books as the ultimate place
Where bad people go, where you end up in disgrace.
It's up to the individual, faith has a hand
Life is as small as a grain of sand.
My belief is that your spirit flies high
As far as it can, free in the sky.
Are we reincarnated? Do we get another chance?
One last attempt at life's long dance.

For other titles from Augur Press
please visit

www.augurpress.com

www.ingramcontent.com/pod-product-compliance
Lightning Source LLC
Chambersburg PA
CBHW051740040426
42447CB00008B/1238